VOICES
at the
CROSSROADS

VOICES
at the
CROSSROADS

First-person, dramatic portrayals
of witnesses to Jesus' death and resurrection

Edited by Paul K. Peterson

Augsburg ✦ Minneapolis

Prayer from *Prayers of Peter Marshall*, edited by Catherine Marshall, copyright © 1949, 1950, 1951, 1954, renewed 1982. Published by Chosen Books, Fleming H. Revell Company. Used by permission.

Prayer from *Gitanjali* by Rabindranath Tagore (New York: Collier Books/Macmillan, 1971). Reprinted by permission.

Scripture quotations are from the New Revised Standard Version Bible, copyright © 1989 by the Division of Christian Education of the National Council of the Churches of Christ in the United States of America. Used with permission.

Cover design and illustration: Catherine Reishus McLaughlin

Library of Congress Cataloging-in-Publication Data

Voices at the crossroads : first-person, dramatic portrayals of
    witnesses to Jesus' death and resurrection / Paul K. Peterson,
    editor.
       p.   cm.
    ISBN 0-8066-2575-9 (alk. paper)
       1. Holy Week services.   2. Jesus Christ—Passion.   3. Jesus
    Christ—Resurrection.   4. Christian drama, American.   5. Bible
    plays, American.   6. Monologues.   7. Lutheran Church—Liturgy—
    Texts.   I. Peterson, Paul K., 1924–   .
    BV90.V65   1991
    232.96—dc20   91-28518
                                                                 CIP

The paper used in this publication meets the minimum requirements of American National Standard for Information Sciences—Permanence of Paper for Printed Library Materials, ANSI Z329.48-1984. ∞ ™

Manufactured in the U.S.A.   AF 9-2575

95   94   93   92   91   1   2   3   4   5   6   7   8   9   10

Contents

Suggestions for Use

These nine dramatic, first-person portrayals of witnesses to the events of Holy Week can be used in services of worship, for special events, and for study groups. The congregation in which these developed used some of them for midweek Lenten services, but the resources in this book would be suitable for other settings as well.

Each soliloquy is based on one or more passages from the Bible. These passages are printed after the soliloquies and are followed by discussion questions. Whatever the context for the soliloquies, those listening will gain much from participating in a discussion of the Bible passages and the issues that were raised in the soliloquies. The discussion questions may be duplicated for group use in congregations if the guidelines on the copyright page in this book are followed.

In the congregation that used these presentations for midweek Lenten services, a short thirty-five-minute service was held in the church, using the brief worship service found on page 67 in this book. The soliloquies were presented from a lectern in the front of the church rather than from the pulpit. After the service, everyone gathered in the fellowship hall in small groups for a twenty-minute discussion period.

In many congregations, soliloquies of this kind have traditionally been presented with the characters dressed in New Testament-era clothing. This is certainly one way to use the materials in this book. However, to help listeners recognize that the feelings of the characters presented are not unique to those who knew Jesus in the first century, the speakers may be costumed in contemporary clothing— for example, army fatigues for the centurion, a business suit and briefcase for Simon, and a black or dark-colored mourning dress for Mary, the mother of Jesus. This is how the soliloquies that follow were originally presented.

Preface

Each year that passes moves us further and further from the events and the people of that critical week in Christian history when Jesus Christ was the victim of the mock justice that led to his execution. Over those years the church has paid scant attention to the feelings of those who were close to Jesus, and to those who were witnesses to his death. More often, we have seen those people as we look back through the surprise and joy of the resurrection that tends to obscure their immediate reaction to the shock of the crucifixion.

The three writers who contributed to this series met to consider the mood and feelings of those who were figures in the high drama of those days. It became clear that those two days were filled with doubt and fear and despair for many of the people who were caught briefly in the spotlight of the passion story of our Lord.

We decided to pick out five of those minor characters (four more were added later) and try to portray their feelings in the gloom of that day that we post-Easter Christians now call "Good Friday" and the day immediately following. Thus, our attempt was to explore how each of these people must have felt immediately after the crucifixion—before their faith was confirmed or strengthened by the resurrection. In choosing to limit our reflection to those two days, we felt we were able to address some of the doubts and fears of many people—those who still wonder about the reality of the new life that Christians claim for themselves, and those who are part of the household of faith who in times of stress frequently echo the prayer of the father of the epileptic boy, "I believe; help my unbelief!" (Mark 9:24)

It should be noted that two of the soliloquies in this collection do not fit into the time frame just described. The presentation by Judas is really an address and challenge to the church, and may be useful as a meditation for a Good Friday service. The second soliloquy of Mary Magdalene can be used on Easter Sunday or in the Easter season. In it, Mary deals with her discovery of the risen Christ and with the reaction of the disciples to her dramatic announcement of the resurrection.

1

The Centurion
Based on Mark 15:37-45

I suppose the reason I was asked to come here tonight has to do with the fact that I was the Roman officer in charge at the crucifixion of the Galilean—this Jesus who had that ridiculous sign nailed over his cross that said he was the king of the Jews. Now, I've commanded the cohort of legionaires at more than a few crucifixions, but this is the first time I have been in charge of the crucifixion of a king! But, I must say, there wasn't much about this character that was very kingly when he died . . . except for that crown of branches from the thorn tree. Oh, my men made some fun of him before we started for that godforsaken hill where he died. They dressed him up in a makeshift king's robe made of a piece of purple cloth, and they gave him some fake homage like they would a king. But they took that purple rag away when it began to be soaked with the blood from his back where he had been scourged. It wasn't a pretty sight . . . but these crucifixions never are.

The troops fairly regularly take out their anger on the prisoners before they die. And they are angry. They're angry at being stationed out here in this miserable outpost of the empire. Most of them are far from home, and mad at Rome for shipping them out here, so they take out their frustration on any convenient target. It's not hard to understand, you know. Most of the hundred men in my cohort never enlisted in the legion. They're people who've been drafted—"forcefully recruited" we say—from other provinces in the empire. Not that I'm apologizing for them, or am ashamed of them. Most of them have turned out to be pretty good soldiers. But this week in this city has been tough, tougher than it was last year at this time. There's a creeping mood of rebellion among some of the locals, and the governor is plainly nervous. No wonder he asked for reinforcements for our legion. You should have seen him at the trial of this Jesus. It almost made me ashamed to be a Roman citizen. He flatly caved in to the crowd and let them have their way. He released a known, convicted murderer and insurrectionist at their demand, and sentenced this guy who had no hard evidence against him at all to death.

I overlooked that at first. After all, he's the governor, and he has Caesar's commission to run this place. He gives the orders to my tribune, my tribune gives the order to me and the other centurions, and we give the orders to the men in our cohorts. I understand the chain of command, and if I want a promotion after my hitch in this place is over, I'd better not mess it up. You get my point? I've been in this man's army for ten years, and have waited six of those ten years before I was promoted to centurion. I enlisted—and I also volunteered for duty in this place. But now I'm beginning to wish I hadn't.

You see, I'm a loyal Roman. I was born in Rome. I have been a part of the expansion of the empire. Caesar is the closest thing I have ever known to a god. And I've been loyal to Caesar. But certain things have happened out here in this wasteland, things that shouldn't bother me . . . things I can't understand. I don't know if I can explain them, but let me try.

We get out on the street a lot. The governor wants to be sure the Roman presence is obvious in Jerusalem during these days. There's some kind of religious festival going on. The locals do this every year. People come from all over the empire to be here for it. Last Sunday we were on patrol in the city when there was a minor ruckus at one of the city gates. A small crowd of people surrounded this Jesus—the one we just executed today—as he came riding into the city on a donkey. They were shouting and carrying on like he was a conquering king. But truthfully he looked kind of silly sitting on that donkey with people throwing branches in his pathway. They were shouting at him, shouting at anyone who would listen. It was all in their native language, and I only know a few phrases, but it was something about him being the son of their great King David who lived centuries ago.

I didn't think too much about it, except for the comedy of it. The crowd dispersed quickly enough and the troops didn't have to break it up. But the next day we were sent over to their temple. It seems that this Jesus had created some trouble over there, within the temple walls. He had torn the place up all by himself and run off some of the merchants who were selling animals and pigeons for their ritual sacrifices. But again, the crowd dispersed quickly, and things calmed down.

But you could tell there was trouble brewing. It hung in the air like the smell of camel dung. The troops could sense it too. Maybe that's what triggered some of their anger at this Jesus when we were ordered to do the scourging. I don't know.

I suppose I would have forgotten all about those incidents earlier in the week if it hadn't been for today. My cohort was on duty at the praetorium this morning. The local religious officials brought in this Jesus and demanded that the governor try him for claiming he was king of the Jews. He had already been worked over pretty well; they apparently had had some kind of mock trial of their own. Well, I've already told you what happened. The governor was so scared of a rebellion he caved in to the crowd. But I couldn't keep my eyes off this Jesus. For a man being framed by a mob he was so quiet. He scarcely spoke. He might have been scared, but it didn't show. He just kept silent; he simply wouldn't be provoked. And that's different, let me tell you. I've been around at other trials like this, and I've heard people who were as guilty as sin cry and whine like babies when they faced this kind of sentence. It wasn't as if he didn't know what was going on . . . but there was no crying, no appeal for mercy . . . nothing, just silence.

Well, after my men had done the required scourging, and had their fun with the purple robe and all that, we made our way out of there toward the crucifixion hill—Calvary it's called—"Calvarium," the skull. That's sure an appropriate name. We had a little incident along the way. He fell, and couldn't get up, so a couple of my men ordered someone out of the crowd to pick up the timber and carry it for him to the hill.

I was at the end of the column, and by the time I got to the site my men were already about their business. I went up to make sure the ropes were in place and the nailing was going all right when I heard him mutter something like, "Father forgive them, for they don't know what they are doing." I told you I'm not all that good at the language, but I think that's what he said. Well, my men knew what they were doing all right, but forgive them? What kind of criminal was this?

But we had the duty. Orders from the governor are the same as orders from Caesar. But once he was on the cross a couple of things happened that make me wonder. There were people around him. Some of them were obviously his enemies, but there was another group, too. Not too close . . . but they were clearly friends or sympathizers. All women, except for one man. That's strange. Crucifixions are not only cruel and deadly, they're also humiliating. As many of these crucifixions as I have seen, I had never ever seen anyone around who was sympathetic to the criminal. Most people—even family—stay away from these things. They can't afford to be associated with the one being executed for fear that they will become suspect, too. But these women hung on to the very end.

And another thing . . . it's customary for us to give the dying some relief with a drug to kill the pain. It's a horrible way to die, and we Romans do have some feeling for that pain, you know. But Jesus refused the drug. It's as if he wanted the pain—he wanted to experience the pain. I've never seen that before either! There was something about him . . . something almost noble . . . something about the dignity he managed to hold on to during the trial, that word forgiving my men when they nailed him, the refusal of the drug—and then there was that eerie darkness as if heaven were in mourning.

And how about the loyalty of that little group of women? I could almost understand that part—loyalty is something I know about. But I wonder if I could be that loyal to Caesar if the chips were down. . .

The final straw was when he died. Just as it was clear he was about to breathe his last he cried out, but it wasn't a cry of pain. It was more like a cry of accomplishment—of fulfillment—as if he had done what he was supposed to do. And then he died. Yes, he did die. It was my job to certify that he was dead, and he was dead. But it wasn't like the others. Oh, he was as dead as the others, but this one . . . well, I said at the time that this one was the Son of God. I'm not sure I even know what that means. I've never been very religious—Caesar and the legion, that's been my religion. But

I'm not sure I'll ever get over this—this feeling, this experience. I've got a lot of questions, and I don't know where or when I'll get any answers.

Mark 15:37-45

Then Jesus gave a loud cry and breathed his last. And the curtain of the temple was torn in two, from top to bottom. Now when the centurion, who stood facing him, saw that in this way he breathed his last, he said, "Truly this man was God's Son!"

There were also women looking on from a distance; among them were Mary Magdalene, and Mary the mother of James the younger and of Joses, and Salome. These used to follow him and provided for him when he was in Galilee; and there were many other women who had come up with him to Jerusalem.

When evening had come, and since it was the day of Preparation, that is, the day before the sabbath, Joseph of Arimathea, a respected member of the council, who was also himself waiting expectantly for the kingdom of God, went boldly to Pilate and asked for the body of Jesus. Then Pilate wondered if he were already dead; and summoning the centurion, he asked him whether he had been dead for some time. When he learned from the centurion that he was dead, he granted the body to Joseph.

Questions for Reflection
and Discussion

1. What is the tone of the passage from Mark 15:37-45? How does the mood change from verse 37 to verse 45?

2. Notice that quite a few people are included in these few verses. What role did the centurion play in the interaction between Pilate and Joseph of Arimathea?

3. The Gospel of Mark uses powerful descriptive words and phrases. Take note of the way these add information and feeling to the story: "a loud cry," "from top to bottom," "truly," "from a distance," "waiting expectantly," and "went boldly." If you are using a different version, check to see how these same words and phrases are stated there.

4. Who in our age might be the counterpart of the centurion?

5. How might questions be a sign of strength of faith, rather than a sign of weakness?

6. Can you identify times in your own life when belief was difficult to hang on to?

2

Mary Magdalene
Based on Luke 8:1-3
and Matthew 27:55-56

I **didn't really** want to come here tonight. I don't think I'm ready to talk to you. Everything that has happened in the last few days has left me so confused, I—I need some time to sort it out. I'm in no condition to offer testimony on anyone's behalf—least of all his. I mean Jesus, of course.

You know, don't you? . . . He's dead! They killed him this afternoon like a common criminal. Mocked him. Scorned him. Put him on "trial." What a joke! That was no trial, it was a public show for Pilate's benefit . . . and it worked! They led Jesus away like a wounded animal carrying his own cross. I can't believe it even now, though I saw it with my own eyes. I keep hoping against all hope that this is only a terrible nightmare out of which I'd waken and find Jesus still alive. But that is not the case. Jesus is dead. I saw his body as they took him from the cross. I helped to dress him in the grave cloths. I kissed his cold, lifeless hand—his hands that had so often touched us with his gentle love!

Why? Why did he let them take him? He didn't try to escape. He didn't resist. He almost seemed to be waiting for them. Is this what he was trying to tell us before we came to Jerusalem? Did he know? And if Jesus knew, why didn't he tell us? After all, we were his friends. We've followed him for all of this time. We believed in him. And we would have saved him! But he didn't even give us

17

would too. But I was wrong. Oh, the euphoria did wear off and life did get ordinary again, but never hopeless. And what I found was that as I began to live in his love, I felt freer and freer to love others. We were a motley bunch, I guess, wandering the hillsides, following the Master—a few faithful followers who had been touched by his love. But I didn't feel outrageous anymore or useless or hopeless. I felt real. I felt like I had an identity all my own. And I knew he loved me simply because I was me! I can't describe that heady freedom I felt with him except to say he gave me back my life.

But now that he is gone some of the old fears are coming back. I suppose that's why I'm so confused. And that's why I didn't want to talk to you tonight. Don't you see? He was so important to me when he was right here and I could touch him and see him, listen to his voice and follow him. I was so certain then that what he said was the truth that God wanted us to hear. And now, I find myself shaky in his absence. Is my faith in what he said and did so weak that it can't outlive this outrageous death on a cross? Why did he abandon us without even so much as a fight? Didn't he know how much we need him?

It's strange though. In the middle of all of this shakiness, somehow I do not feel hopeless. That's strange, isn't it? Here, when the very person who taught me to hope again lies dead in a tomb, I can still say that within me I have hope. Something is working in me just as though he were here, right now. Can what he said continue to be true? Can it be that his forgiveness stretches even beyond the grave?

Everything seems to go back to that moment, doesn't it? And to his forgiveness. Yes. That was the beginning for me. From that time on I began to take on confidence that I was somebody who mattered. I began to know who I was. And I won't let this terrible Friday take that away from me! I had something to live for before he died. I must hang on to that somehow. But for now, I would rather be left alone to cry out my grief. I have no idea where I will go from here. Magdala is not my home any longer. And certainly I won't stay in this blood-stained city.

You see, this is not a good time for us to be talking. Though it has helped me to remember him and what he meant to me, I am not prepared to give a public statement in his defense. All I know is that he rescued me from the hell that I was living in and he gave me a reason to live. And somehow his forgiving me set me free to love and to be loved. I can't say I understand it all, but I do know that Jesus worked this change in me.

Can you understand then, how frightening this moment is for me? Perhaps when I'm thinking more clearly I'll have more to say. But not now. I'm sorry. I must go and find the others. We need to be together in our grief tonight.

Luke 8:1-3

Soon afterwards he went on through cities and villages, proclaiming and bringing the good news of the kingdom of God. The twelve were with him, as well as some women who had been cured of evil spirits and infirmities: Mary called Magdalene, from whom seven demons had gone out, and Joanna, the wife of Herod's steward Chuza, and Susanna, and many others, who provided for them out of their resources.

Matthew 27:55, 56

Many women were also there, looking on from a distance; they had followed Jesus from Galilee and had provided for him. Among them were Mary Magdalene, and Mary the mother of James and Joseph, and the mother of the sons of Zebedee.

Questions for Reflection and Discussion

1. Jesus had healed Mary Magdalene from demon possession. What do you suppose she was like before she was healed?

2. How was Jesus' response to disabled or rejected people different from the world's response to them? What is your response?

3. Mary Magdalene was one of many women who were followers of Jesus. Notice in Luke 8:3 what role some of them played in Jesus' ministry.

4. Galilee is some distance north of Jerusalem, yet the women had left their homes in Galilee to care for Jesus' needs. What does this say about their faith; also about their courage, considering the subservient roles women were supposed to play at that time?

5. What do you think about the fact that the women stayed at the crucifixion until after Jesus died, even though many others left?

3

Simon of Cyrene
Based on Mark 15:16-27

I have been asked to come here to tell you about what happened yesterday. I can tell you this—it was one of the strangest, most disturbing days of my life. Something happened to me that I shall never forget. In fact, it already seems to me that I won't want to forget what happened. And not only will I remember it—the story is still so upsetting—that I'm reasonably certain I will tell of it many times again, even though it's such a grim and painful story that I really should want to forget that it ever happened to me.

But first, let me tell you something about myself. I'm a stranger in these parts, just as I was a stranger in Jerusalem yesterday. My name is Simon, and my home is in Cyrene—that's a city that is part of a Roman province in Africa, on the coast—south across the sea from the city of Corinth in Greece. It may seem strange to you that I happened to be in Jerusalem yesterday. That's a long way from home. Actually, I was in Jerusalem on business. Well, sort of on business. My family has been in the export business in Cyrene for years and years. My great-grandfather emigrated from Israel—well, actually fled from Israel during a time of persecution—and started a new life on a tiny farm. He did well, as did my grandfather and father. The crop they planted and cared for is called silphium—a product that is in great demand as a spice with certain medicinal properties. My father started in the export business, shipping silphium to communities in a wider and wider circle. Now the business is mine, and I, together with my sons Alexander and Rufus, are looking to expand our markets. And that's what brought me to Jerusalem. Well, to be honest, it's not the only thing that brought me to Jerusalem. I've already mentioned that my ancestors are Jewish and so am I. Even though we have been removed from our homeland for generations, we have remained faithful children of Abraham and Sarah. Ever since my great-grandfather left the homeland, not one of our family has returned, although we have faithfully paid the half-shekel temple tax all these years. My idea was to combine this business trip with a trip to the holy city at Passover, and be the first of the descendants to be in Jerusalem for the great feast. Besides, everyone knows that pilgrims come from all over the world at this time of year. The city grows from a population of 50,000 to 250,000 during this holy season. The opportunities for contacts with importers in every port around the sea would be enormous. That's just good business, isn't it?

Well, it started out to be good business anyway. Yesterday morning I had just finished having a cup of coffee with a potential client and was starting across town to the room I had managed to find with the help of a friend, when, all of a sudden the Romans held up traffic for a parade of prisoners who were on their way to execution outside the city. They were on their way to be crucified. I tried to break through the police lines and be on my way, but this centurion held me back, and there I was in the front row for the parade. It's never a pretty sight. We had seen plenty of these barbaric executions done by the Romans at home, and I had no desire to have anything to do with this one. But all of a sudden, one of the three prisoners stumbled right in front of me. He was a mess. It was clear he had been worked over pretty badly. My first impulse was to help the poor guy up, but he was covered with blood, had welts and open wounds on his back, and a crazy crown made from branches of a thorn tree around his head. His face was awash with blood. I didn't even want to look at him, his appearance was so grisly. But the guy couldn't get up, and the beam he was carrying seemed almost to pin him to the ground. And before I knew it, two of those Roman guards grabbed me out of the crowd and told me to pick up the beam and follow along. Well, I knew very well that you don't mess with those Romans. My protest was swallowed before I spoke it. I had good clothes on, and here I was told to carry the beam for this guy's cross. As I picked it up off his back, he looked at me as he was struggling to his feet. I remember that. He looked at me. He didn't say anything—he just looked at me, and in that look was more than gratitude. I don't know what it was, but despite his appearance, with all that blood and that crazy crown on his head, that look touched me so deeply that any thought I had of further resistance just left my mind.

We didn't have much farther to go to get to the hill where the crucifixion would be done. Leave it to these Romans to find an obvious, public place to do their deadly business! I decided to hang around to see what would happen. Oh, everything proceeded just as all crucifixions do—the ropes, the nails, and all the rest. Did I say there were three of them? The crowd standing around told me that the other two were thieves and were being crucified as an example to the city. But this one whose beam I carried was being crucified for sedition. He didn't look like a dangerous seditionist to me, and that little knot of people—mostly women—who seemed to be his friends certainly didn't look like dangerous rebels!

Even though that look he gave me back there in the street still haunted me, I was about to leave and get on with my business contacts and prepare myself to enjoy the Passover, when some strange things happened. The sky grew darker—not like a storm though. It seemed more like an eclipse, except that it wasn't that. I don't know what it was. He spoke a few times, but I wasn't close enough to hear what he said, except for one thing. He quoted a Psalm—he said, "My God, my God, why have you forsaken me?" Strange that he quoted that, isn't it? If he was a criminal, I would have expected an appeal for mercy either from Caesar or from God— or some last-ditch confession.

Well, my curiosity got the best of me and I began to ask some questions of this little group of women who were obviously his friends. I found out his name was Jesus. He was from Nazareth— some little burg up north. He had been traveling around the territory preaching and had done some amazing things, and some of the people were believing that he was the Messiah. Imagine that! That probably explains the sign they printed and hung over his head that said he was the king of the Jews, but if he were the Messiah, the big shots from the temple wouldn't have been in the crowd that hung around the cross taunting him and giving him a bad time. But something about him, and something about the sincerity of those few women who were with him really unsettled me. Maybe it was that look he gave me back there on the street. Maybe it was something about the way he managed to maintain some sense of dignity even while he was in the middle of the pain of his crucifixion. Maybe it was the change in the sky—as if God were angry, or maybe sorrowing over what was happening. I don't know.

In any event, it didn't take long for him to die. It's not surprising. He had lost so much blood from the beatings he had gotten. I left just as they were taking him down, and someone had volunteered a tomb for him because it was getting late and the sabbath was about to begin.

Well, I went to the Passover last night. As much as I had looked forward to it—as often as I had said, "Next year in Jerusalem," I couldn't get my mind off this Jesus who died. He was in my thoughts as the lessons were read. He was in my thoughts as we ate the meal. The thought that kept nagging at me was "What if those women were right?"

One more thing—this morning I heard that there had been an appeal to the governor and a guard had been placed at the tomb where they buried him. Now that's strange! Why would they guard the tomb of a dead criminal? I don't know, except . . . well . . .

My plan was to start for home tomorrow and stop to see some clients on the way. I have a reservation on a ship that will stop in Corinth and in Crete before it gets to Cyrene. But something tells me that it's too soon to leave. I think I'll change my reservations and hang around Jerusalem for a couple of days, and see if I can talk to some others about this Jesus. The story doesn't seem really complete in my mind. It sounds foolish, I know. He's probably just another nut who thinks he's the Messiah. On the other hand, I just can't stop thinking about him. Besides, I may run across someone who might be a prospect for our silphium. At any rate, I'll have a story to tell to Rufus and Alexander when I get home: the story of my first Passover in Jerusalem, and the new business I found on the way.

You'll have to excuse me now. I have a date for coffee with a couple of those women I met out on that hill. Maybe they'll be able to introduce me to someone who will tell me something that will help me make sense of all this stuff that's troubling me.

Mark 15:16-27

Then the soldiers led him into the courtyard of the palace (that is, the governor's headquarters); and they called together the whole cohort. And they clothed him in a purple cloak; and after twisting some thorns into a crown, they put it on him. And they began saluting him, "Hail, King of the Jews!" They struck his head with a reed, spat upon him, and knelt down in homage to him. After mocking him, they stripped him of the purple cloak and put his own clothes on him. Then they led him out to crucify him.

They compelled a passer-by, who was coming in from the country, to carry his cross; it was Simon of Cyrene, the father of Alexander and Rufus. Then they brought Jesus to the place called Golgotha (which means the place of a skull). And they offered him wine mixed with myrrh; but he did not take it. And they crucified him, and divided his clothes among them, casting lots to decide what each should take.

It was nine o'clock in the morning when they crucified him. The inscription of the charge against him read, "The King of the Jews." And with him they crucified two bandits, one on his right and one on his left.

Questions for Reflection
and Discussion

1. Notice that we are given the names of Simon's sons, Alexander and Rufus. What does this add to the account? Why do you think this information was included?

2. How would you have felt if you had been watching the grim scene of the soldiers mocking Jesus who was in great pain and weak from loss of blood? Would you have been able to stay or would you have tried to leave?

3. Simon went home from Jerusalem a changed person with a story to tell. How does that desire to tell the story of Jesus continue through the church in the world, and through your own life?

4. Who might Simon's counterparts be in our age?

5. How do you deal with new challenges and new insights into your faith life?

Voices at the Crossroads, edited by Paul K. Peterson.
Copyright © 1991 Augsburg Fortress.
This page may be reproduced for local use.

4.

Pilate's Wife
Based on Matthew 27:15-24

I'm not sure I should be here, out on this lonely night. The town of Jerusalem seems overtaken by some kind of fear—or some expectation of fear. I don't know what it is, but I can feel it around me, suffocating me.

Since the day he rode into town, I've felt it—the people pressing in on one another to hear him, everyone talking about him—even the servants. And that motley bunch of followers shouting his praises—that kind of spectacle disgusts me. But for some reason, I had to hear him too. Oh, if my husband, the governor, ever knew that I had been one of the anonymous faces in the crowd listening to Jesus, he would be furious. But he haunts me—this Jesus. His words attack my spirit and challenge my thinking and it is driving me mad!

I told my husband more than once to have nothing to do with Jesus. The man from Nazareth has invaded my dreams, and all I see is that wounded face. But no! No one listens to me. After all, I am only the governor's wife. My opinion counts for nothing. It's no different today than it ever was. I am simply the hostess of the palace, a decorative touch for the proper occasions, and I am to be content with a life of insignificant details that lead to . . . nothing! It is no wonder my voice, my life carries no merit except as a possession of the governor.

There was a time when it was not so—or at least I didn't feel it so directly. We had hopes and dreams that we shared, my husband

and I. When we were young we would take endless walks and spin
our dreams out in words that would excite us both. We laughed a
lot then and we seemed to have a way of reaching each other. We
really cared. I'm not sure about now. I think it's still there in us,
but it's hidden—maybe buried—by so many of the pressures of life
in Jerusalem. Why am I thinking about this now?

I know why. It's because Jesus' words set me back into those
feelings of being free to dream again. To hope, for something more.
I was drawn to him like a magnet, responding to his words as though
they spoke what was inside of me. How could he know? How could
that poor carpenter from Nazareth have known what is working in
me or what has been buried there for so long? Was he some kind
of wizard or sorcerer? Or a false prophet working to stir up the
people of Jerusalem into some kind of mad frenzy? Well, whatever
he was, it's over now—all of this madness. Jesus is dead, and his
body has been sealed in a tomb somewhere.

I watched what I could from the balcony, though the crowds
were so thick I could hardly see him from where I stood. But he
fell once and the crowd backed away for a moment, and then I saw
him. What a pitiful sight. How could they do that to him? He may
not have been what he claimed to be—the king of the Jews—but
he had done nothing to warrant that kind of treatment. Even my
husband couldn't stand to see it. He turned away, and busied himself
with other things. But I watched that awful parade until my eyes
could no longer make out his body hunched over and carrying that
wretched cross. They said that when he couldn't take it any longer,
someone else was forced to carry it for him. Can you imagine having
to do that? Poor soul . . .

I couldn't go up there—to Golgotha. I couldn't watch that sight.
It's barbaric. How could they do that to him? How could they be
so cruel? What had he done? I told him. I did. I told my husband
to leave him alone because . . . because he was innocent. He was
more than innocent. I knew that, and so did the governor. But we
didn't have the power—or the courage—to stop it.

And so, he died. For no good reason, he died. The sky went
black as though the sun was raging against this injustice. Was that
his God making his displeasure known? Perhaps so.

I don't know why, but this man, Jesus, has touched my life and
I am sickened by his death. I wonder how many others are walking

around the city today feeling the same way, afraid to tell anyone for fear they'll be accused of being disloyal to the Roman guard.

Hope. I think that's what I saw in him. Hope for us, coming out of a gentle confidence in himself. He spoke—about my own life, it seemed—in words that touched my heart and excited me. I don't know why, I only saw him from far off—but I felt as though he knew what it was like to feel insignificant and unimportant. And he was telling me that I mattered. In this whole grand scheme of things where men are busy plotting one thing and then the next, I matter. That gives me hope. Maybe there is something more to my life than simply being the governor's pampered and protected wife. He didn't give idle advice, this Jesus. He just gave me such a sense of . . . of being whole and valuable—and loved.

How can a perfect stranger come so close? I haven't talked about love to anyone for ages. It seemed to be a lost cause. Love is for romance and quickly fades. But Jesus talked about love as though it were here—in our lives—whenever we cared to look for it. And he said that because of this love we could love one another better. How can he be so certain about something you can't even see or touch—or feel? But I believed him. He knows about a love that I have longed for, but have never known. And, strangely enough, he says it's mine.

No wonder he haunts my dreams. He has invaded my life with his hope and his talk about love. Is that his crime? That he wants us to believe that such things are possible in our lives and that there is a better way to live with one another? His message doesn't fit this world very well. But everyone who was in that crowd that day seemed to be desperate to hear it.

What have they done? There is a sick and sinking feeling in me that says we have just watched our last chance for hope die on a cross. And I—I am afraid to dream tonight.

Matthew 27:15-24

Now at the festival the governor was accustomed to release a prisoner for the crowd, anyone whom they wanted. At that time they had a notorious prisoner, called Jesus Barabbas. So after they had gathered, Pilate said to them, "Whom do you want me to release for you, Jesus Barabbas or Jesus who is called the Messiah?" For he realized that it was out of jealousy that they had handed him over.

While he was sitting on the judgment seat, his wife sent word to him, "Have nothing to do with that innocent man, for today I have suffered a great deal because of a dream about him." Now the chief priests and the elders persuaded the crowds to ask for Barabbas and to have Jesus killed. The governor again said to them, "Which of the two do you want me to release for you?" And they said, "Barabbas." Pilate said to them, "Then what should I do with Jesus who is called the Messiah?" All of them said, "Let him be crucified!" Then he asked, "Why, what evil has he done?" But they shouted all the more, "Let him be crucified!"

So when Pilate saw that he could do nothing, but rather that a riot was beginning, he took some water and washed his hands before the crowd, saying, "I am innocent of this man's blood; see to it yourselves."

Questions for Reflection and Discussion

1. Dreams often play important roles in events described in the Bible. In the stories surrounding Jesus' birth in Matthew, dreams are mentioned five times: 1:20; 2:12, 13, 19, 22. Pilate's wife took her dream very seriously; did Pilate?

2. What conflicting voices were trying to get Pilate's attention? Which ones did he finally listen to?

3. In this soliloquy, Pilate's wife felt drawn to Jesus and his teachings. When and how does commitment to something new challenge our loyalties?

4. Pilate's wife is depicted as longing for a closer relationship with her husband as in their earlier days when they found ways to express their caring. How do important relationships erode into staleness?

5. How does new faith rekindle old hope?

5

Joseph of Arimathea
Based on Luke 23:50-56

I am troubled, deeply troubled. Judging from the cross so boldly emblazoned everywhere you know something about the occupying army and its presence in my homeland. I am not sure who you are. Either you are fanatics dedicated to the cruelty of this capital punishment or you are some group I do not yet understand.

I cannot comprehend why someone would glorify such a hideous means of death but then I am not afraid to speak out. I am a leader of my people. I am one of the seventy, the Sanhedrin, and it is my joy to address issues before which others cringe. I have gone to the governor himself when it was necessary. I am Joseph of Arimathea, and I am unashamed to admit I am a Jew. I don't know why you are here, but I am here to pay final respects to my rabbi who has been killed on your cross.

Perhaps you have heard about Jesus. Then you know you have not found my name on the list of his twelve followers. You haven't heard of me in connection with the seventy who went out in his name either. Jesus touched a broad spectrum of people. He reached out to both Jews and non-Jews—like Samaritans. He ate with Pharisees as well as with tax collectors. He welcomed Roman soldiers and zealots. He connected with the rich and poor alike. He loved the religious and the secular without distinction. He associated with old and young, with men and women. He had friends who were shepherds and friends who were religious leaders. He befriended humankind in its diversity. But all of us have one thing in common.

We warmed to his love. We have been willing to be met by God not just on the Sabbath but during the week as well; not just in the Torah but in a love powerful enough to keep all of the law; not just in the sacrifice of lambs and turtledoves but in the sacrificial living of Jesus of Nazareth.

I say this because at one time I was slow to find my tongue. As a political and religious leader I have learned the necessity of being above reproach. I have learned to be circumspect in my connections with those who could cause offense. I never admitted that Jesus was my rabbi until it was too late. The vote was being cast and there was only a handful of us who dared to speak against the sacrifice of this holy man. The majority of us wanted to do anything to keep Rome off our back just a little while longer. Nicodemus was another and the honored Gamaliel also. We each had our own reasons but they were not sufficient to sway Caiaphas the High Priest and the rest. Their minds were made up.

I know Jesus believed in the resurrection of the dead. I believed too. How could I have done otherwise when the authority with which he preached and taught and healed demonstrated the ultimate triumph of good over evil? But I never knew the finality of death until now, until I got my hands bloodied with his burial. I came to believe Jesus was God's elect sent to bring us life. And he was full of life. You would not believe the stories I could tell about those who were healed even at death's door by him. Children and slaves and lepers and the lame, even those who had already died like Lazarus can swear of his power and might. There were those of us who not only hoped but trusted that he was the Christ of God, the Messiah whom the Lord sent to save us from our sins. Yet we, the leaders of Israel, voted to turn God's elect over to the Romans to be executed on their pagan cross. My voice could not stem the tide. It was done.

Injustice and hatred have kissed. Violence and jealousy hold hands. I didn't know a body could be so broken. I hadn't realized how much blood one person has. I was unaware pain and death could twist and contort like they do. Unless I had known him in life I wouldn't have recognized him in death. He had fed empty stomachs, had given sight to the blind, had blessed instead of cursed, had forgiven instead of judged. Where were these healed people, these witnesses of Jesus' miracle, when Satan grinned with delight? Where were the families who were given loved ones back alive when the sky clouded over? Where was mercy, or just plain common decency, when the nails were struck? Where was God when he was buried?

That was when I found my tongue. It no longer mattered to me that the High Festival was going on. I was glad to make myself ritually unclean, unfit to celebrate the Passover. I went to the Roman Pilate's home. I asked for the privilege of taking the body down and burying it. You see, in our culture the only death which is accursed is death on a tree. Those killed in this way are the ones who die separated from the promise made to father Abraham. The bodies of those executed on the cross often remain impaled for days and weeks after their death. It is a grisly reminder of the consequences of breaking the law. I have seen fathers hoist their young ones on their shoulders to see. I have heard them say, "Don't you ever end up like that!"

Jesus was a good man. He was filled with the goodness of God. I couldn't stop his death, but I was not about to let him rot on a cross. It is ironic. He who identified himself so closely with those who had nothing during their life has now ended up being one with those who have lost everything in death. He who made himself unclean with the diseases of his people is now unclean with their death. I could not live with myself if I also didn't make myself unclean by touching him gently, respectfully, and with love.

So I buried him. I placed him in my own grave. Nicodemus and I did the final dignities for the man we had come to cherish as our hope. We pried his body from the cross, washed him and laid him in the grave. It was a new tomb. It had never before been used. I clarify this because among my people graves are used again and again. Even as death comes swiftly, so does burial. Because of our climate we cannot afford to postpone interment. We are too poor to embalm as is the custom in some parts of the world. Many who have broken the fast of the night with loved ones in the morning have wept at their graves by sundown. Our graves are caves or sepulchers, and the bodies are left in them until they have decomposed and returned to the earth from which they came. My task is not yet complete. In several years I will return and gather up his bones. I will place them in a box we call an ossuary, and I will find a final resting place for him. This is the custom for burying our dead. When I have done this I finally will have done all I can.

Meanwhile, my rabbi blesses my grave for me. He who taught me to pray has become the prayer making holy this grave I bought for my own use. Nicodemus and I tucked him in as gently as we would a little child at the end of the day. Sleep well, dear friend. In death as in life you touch me. I cannot get away from you. You have reached beyond yourself and have given me the gift of myself. You have made me bold to speak and to act on behalf of love and justice just as you have done. Rest well, dear friend. I thank you for having made me alive.

We left him there. I understand a guard was posted to seal and watch the grave. I don't understand. Even in death they won't leave him alone. But they can no longer harm him. It's obvious they never really heard his message of the true power of love. Their hearts, like so many, are still driven by fear and hate. Of course I cannot go home—at least not for a while. The law forbids anyone defiled by death to return home without first being made clean. And that will take time. I am not sure what I will do or where I will stay. But I don't think I want to be safe in my home now anyway. I don't understand your fascination with the cross but I am seeing it differently than ever before. Jesus said that if any were to come after him we should pick up our cross and follow. It led him to the grave. I wonder where it will lead me.

To my grave, too, I suppose. Jesus won't be in it forever. He will just be using it for a little while. With any luck I won't need it before he is through. By then it won't matter anyway.

Luke 23:50-56

Now there was a good and righteous man named Joseph, who, though a member of the council, had not agreed to their plan and action. He came from the Jewish town of Arimathea, and he was waiting expectantly for the kingdom of God. This man went to Pilate and asked for the body of Jesus. Then he took it down, wrapped it in a linen cloth, and laid it in a rock-hewn tomb where no one had ever been laid. It was the day of Preparation, and the sabbath was beginning. The women who had come with him from Galilee followed, and they saw the tomb and how his body was laid. Then they returned, and prepared spices and ointments.

On the sabbath they rested according to the commandment.

Questions for Reflection and Discussion

1. Notice how Joseph is described in this passage, especially verse 51. What might have been some of the costs of his refusal to go along with the council's decision?

2. Joseph was considered unclean for touching Jesus' dead body. Are there ways you have been willing to risk "uncleanness" on behalf of the love of God?

3. Christianity has been described as the invitation to "risk with grace rather than remain safe with the law." Sometimes a higher call moves us to think beyond the letter of the law. In what ways do you hear this challenge to boldness in our day?

4. Can you describe times when love has compelled costly or unpopular actions on your part instead of simply making you comfortable?

5. For the Christian, grief and faith are not polar opposites. Describe what you would want said at your own funeral.

Voices at the Crossroads, edited by Paul K. Peterson.
Copyright © 1991 Augsburg Fortress.
This page may be reproduced for local use.

6

Mary, the Mother of Jesus
Based on Luke 2:25-40
and John 19:25-27

Of all the people you have met here in this cross-examination, you probably know the most about me—or at least you think you do. I am the one you wrap in the pale blue veils of your Christmas fantasies, dressing up the story of Jesus' birth with your imagination, making it all so lovely. A young, innocent girl chosen by God to bear the Messiah, to carry inside my body the hope of the world.

Well, today that hope is dead. I watched him die—and no powers of your imagination can make this moment lovely. Today, I am shrouded in black, a woman made old by a cruel trick that has been played on me. My son has died a criminal's death, and I do not understand why!

Do you? Do you know why Jesus had to die? In all of your great imaginations have you conjured up a reasonable explanation for this horror of a day? Can you explain for this mother's heart why my son had to die?

I'm sorry. I didn't intend for you to see me like this. I thought I had pulled myself together enough to speak with you. But you see, I'm caught. Yes, caught between what I feel and what I think I ought to be saying to you right now. I feel. . . . crushed—abandoned and confused. But that's not what you want to hear. You don't need a mother's wailing grief, you need to know that there is a reason and a purpose for all of this. And that Jesus' death is not without meaning for you. But the feelings of my heart seem to outweigh the reasoning of my mind tonight. Perhaps I cannot be a very good witness for my own son.

But do you have any idea what my life has been like since he was born? In all of your fantasies about me, have you ever considered the strange mixture of feelings that have accompanied this role that was given to me? When you agree to be the mother of God's son, you make no conditions, no stipulations. You become, instead, inhabited by some kind of holy hope that allows you to believe the unbelievable and somehow accept the miraculous. No more, no less! I never doubted that the child I carried in my womb was any other but God's son. I rejoiced at the great good news that came to me on the lips of an angel, and I laughed with my cousin Elizabeth as her child leaped within her upon my arrival at her home. I offered tears of joy at his birthing even as the pain of releasing him to the world spread through my body and quickened my heart. Yes, I knew that I had borne God's own son. I know. And yet I wondered at the meaning of it all. Why me, Lord? Why was I chosen?

I didn't know it would be like this. I didn't ask for a child who would be so different from the others. But I should have known. There were so many signs. Old Simeon knew. When we brought Jesus to the temple for the first time as an infant, he tried to warn me about this very day, but I could not let myself believe him. What was it he said? "And a sword will pierce your own soul too." How right you were, Simeon. That sword has left its mark on me today.

Oh, there were times when Joseph and I were caught up short by this child. He was loving and gentle and wise beyond his years, but he often seemed preoccupied, almost distant from us. When he was twelve years old, we brought him with us to the Feast of the Passover in Jerusalem. When we began the return trip home, Jesus was nowhere in sight. He stayed there in the temple with the teachers. We didn't know where he was. We assumed he was with the others who made the trip with us. After three days of frantic searching we finally found him back there in Jerusalem, peacefully sitting among the teachers, baffling them with his questions and astounding them with his answers. And all he said to us to explain his behavior was "Did you not know that I must be in my father's house?"

To say I understood then or even now is too far from the truth. I didn't understand, in spite of his miraculous beginning. It was so hard not to make him *my* child—*our* child. I forgot, and when I forgot I seemed to be reminded in ways that tore at my heart. "Woman," he called me at the wedding at Cana—in front of that whole crowd. And at another time when a group of people told him that I was waiting for him, he said to them, "Who is my mother?" You see, he was never really mine at all. He knew it, but I could not accept that gracefully. I knew that he was a part of God's wonderful plan for all of us, but I wanted him as a son, too. Was that so wrong? He never said that it was. Jesus just seemed to love everyone the same—as if all of us were his mother or brother or sister. And I loved him all the more for that.

Do you see how confusing it became for me to understand that my son really wasn't my son? No, he belonged to no one but God. His life was not full of the typical victories and failures of other children. He seemed set on something far different, but I was never able to understand what that was. Oh, I tried and I asked and I kept a lot of my feelings bottled up inside of me, wondering, hoping that some day I would understand and find some peace in all of this.

Hmph. . . . What peace is there to be found now? How can I make any sense out of what they have done to Jesus today? He preached and taught only love. He healed others. And in return for this, he was rejected, beaten, and murdered. Oh, they were afraid of him. I know. I heard the talk in the streets. Caiaphas and his henchmen—they were afraid that Jesus would win the hearts of the people and turn against them. But Jesus was never vindictive—he would never seek to hurt anybody. He only wanted us all to believe that God's way meant life for us—life that was filled with goodness and love.

And I believe that. Jesus was love to me, even though it was a love that sometimes robbed me of my identity as his mother. But I knew his love stretched beyond me and into the lives of others and so I felt joined to all of the people his love touched. I don't understand it . . . but somehow this seemed to be his—his mission, his purpose—joining us all together in this love. When I could stop feeling sorry for myself, when I could take my mind off of what I thought I had lost, I could see that Jesus really was living out what he believed, and I loved him all the more for that.

But that makes this day even harder to understand. I need so desperately to understand something—anything that would give his death some meaning. Is this where it all was supposed to end? Is this what God intended for Jesus? If so, how can I believe in a loving God? Where is that God now? The love has gone out of the world, and it is as dark as the moment he died. And me? I'm afraid that this world will never know light nor love again.

I didn't know that it would come to this—that I would hold this child of mine, a lifeless body mutilated by whips and nails and sword. The hands I held, the sweet face I watched turn into man-hood, now forever still. I tried so hard not to scream out for his pain. As through my tears I watched him slowly die, I felt my own life slowly go out of me. Somehow, he must have known. His eyes found me in the crowd. "Woman," he said, "Here is your son." And he looked right at John then and said "Here is your mother." What was that? His way to tell me to live on? Not to die his death, but to let him die and begin to love again? I have always loved John as long as I have known him, but I doubt that I can ever see him as my son. And yet, this must have been very important to Jesus. He said it so close to the end. I can't sort it out now; it is too soon.

What do I do tonight? What else can a mother do except cry on the night her son dies? Oh, God, I have always believed in your great wisdom for your people, but right now I see none of that wisdom at work in the world. Let there be a sign for us who are left behind. Somehow make this night end and bring us your light and your love again.

I haven't been very helpful to you tonight. I have more questions than answers. Nothing makes any sense to this broken heart I carry in me. Perhaps another day I could be more helpful. But for now, excuse me. I cannot stay here any longer.

Luke 2:25-40

Now there was a man in Jerusalem whose name was Simeon; this man was righteous and devout, looking forward to the consolation of Israel, and the Holy Spirit rested on him. It had been revealed to him by the Holy Spirit that he would not see death before he had seen the Lord's Messiah. Guided by the Spirit, Simeon came into the temple; and when the parents brought in the child Jesus, to do for him what was customary under the law, Simeon took him in his arms and praised God, saying,

> "Master, now you are dismissing
> your servant in peace,
> according to your word;
> for my eyes have seen your
> salvation,
> which you have prepared in
> the presence of all peoples,
> a light for revelation to the
> Gentiles
> and for glory to your people
> Israel."

And the child's father and mother were amazed at what was being said about him. Then Simeon blessed them and said to his mother Mary, "This child is destined for the falling and the rising of many in Israel, and to be a sign that will be opposed so that the inner thoughts of many will be revealed—and a sword will pierce your own soul too."

There was also a prophet, Anna the daughter of Phanuel, of the tribe of Asher. She was of a great age, having lived with her husband seven years after her marriage, then as a widow to the age of eighty-four. She never left the temple but worshiped there with fasting and prayer night and day. At that moment she came, and began to praise God and to speak about the child to all who were looking for the redemption of Jerusalem.

When they had finished everything required by the law of the Lord, they returned to Galilee, to their own town of Nazareth. The child grew and became strong, filled with wisdom; and the favor of God was upon him.

John 19:25-27

Meanwhile, standing near the cross of Jesus were his mother, and his mother's sister, Mary the wife of Clopas, and Mary Magdalene. When Jesus saw his mother and the disciple whom he loved standing beside her, he said to his mother, "Woman, here is your son." Then he said to the disciple, "Here is your mother." And from that hour the disciple took her into his own home.

Questions for Reflection and Discussion

1. God gave Mary and Joseph an enormously important yet somewhat bewildering task: to raise the child Jesus. What do you think Mary's feelings were as Jesus grew and developed?

2. In the soliloquy, Mary referred to Simeon's words that a sword would pierce her soul (Luke 2:35). The prediction was forcefully borne out when Jesus died, but when else might Mary have felt anguish and grief?

3. How do we deal with the problem of knowing in our minds that God is for us, though we feel abandoned and confused at times?

4. How do we best deal with a friend who has lost someone dear and is grieving?

5. How can the church respond with compassion to those who lose loved ones to a violent death?

7

Nicodemus
Based on John 3:1-15; 19:38-42

Well, I suspect it's all over for me now: My place in the community; my seat on the Sanhedrin; my role as teacher. It's all gone now. Yesterday I was forced to take a stand. I wasn't exactly thrilled about it. I still have several more questions than I have answers for, but it couldn't be helped. They crucified him yesterday. Crucified him. For what? He was no criminal. I know the law; I'm a teacher of the law! They simply trumped up charges, and whipped the people into a frenzy. Pilate caved in out of fear and sent an innocent man to the cross. It was *good*, Caiaphas said. "It was good that one man should die for the people." He could at least have been honest when he spoke to us at the council meeting. He should have told us that it was good that this Jesus died to preserve the Sanhedrin's control, or to preserve the tradition that we have inherited from those who have gone before us, or to maintain what little governance we have over our lives in the face of the Roman occupation of our land.

I suppose I should have seen it coming. From the beginning the hostility toward Jesus had been growing among our leadership like a boil under the skin. From our first encounter with him it was plain that a new voice of authority had emerged that would ultimately challenge everything we have always been certain about. Jesus was seen only as a revolutionary by all of us in authority on the Sanhedrin. It had to come to a confrontation. But by the time the confrontation took place there was open hysteria among the

leadership. Oh, a few of us pleaded for fairness—for an opportunity
to hear Jesus out. That had always been the policy of the council—
to hear both sides in any dispute. Not this time. Jesus was too much
of a threat. He didn't have a chance.

Yes, I spoke out against this rush to judgment, and asked why
we didn't take more time to hear from Jesus himself. But I have to
admit that I wasn't very persistent, or very brave. I have a position
to uphold, after all. I have a reputation in my community to protect.
And I wasn't completely convinced myself, but it just seemed to
be so unfair—that we were sacrificing long-standing principles and
procedures out of sheer fear—fear for ourselves and fear for what
Rome might do if an ugly dispute erupted among the people, par-
ticularly with the city as crowded as it is at Passover time.

But there is more to it than that. I have to be honest, at least
to myself. I had met Jesus before—once all by myself. It happened
a couple of years ago very shortly after Jesus of Nazareth came to
be known as a rabbi and as a worker of wonders. Rumors had spread
even as far as Jerusalem that he had developed a following in Galilee.
One incident was widely reported—that he had made water into
wine at a wedding. When he arrived in Jerusalem with his little
band of followers—they really are a scruffy group, fishermen and
country folk and a few members of the Zealot party, no one of any
reputation at all—he tore the temple courtyard apart claiming that
his father's house should not be made a house of trade! His father's
house? What a ridiculous claim—very nearly blasphemous. Yet there
was an earnestness about him that was arresting, a conviction that
caused several of us to question him regarding the authority he had
to make such a claim. I admit that I was more than a little bit
fascinated by him and anxious to pursue my curiosity, so I sought
him out.

It wasn't just idle curiosity that brought me out on that cold and
windy night, however. I came out to visit with Jesus because, as I
said, a group of us had happened to be in conversation in the temple
courtyard when Jesus used a whip to drive the merchants from the
temple grounds. That was a shock, let me tell you! It was the holiest
season of the year, and here this upstart rabbi from up north was
flailing away with this handmade whip, and turning over tables and
scattering the merchants' profits all over the ground. It was a sen-
sational moment. Oh, I might add that for some of us this crass

merchandising of items for sacrifice and money-changing had become offensive, but it was the obvious determination and the ring of authority in Jesus' voice that convinced us that this was more than just a ruse on the part of some young rabbi to gather a following. We questioned him at some length, and he was convincing. He knew the tradition. He knew the law. But he also spoke in mysterious terms about rebuilding the temple in three days. Surely this was a figure of speech, though no one could understand what he meant.

After that conversation it was agreed among the few of us there who are members of the Sanhedrin—the council—that we wanted to know more about this strange but compelling person. I was deputized by the group—well, actually I volunteered—to seek him out and question him further.

I found him that night outside, all alone. The wind was blowing. It was cold and dark. I was relieved to find him alone. After all, I am a respected member of the party of the Pharisees, and considered the ranking teacher of the people. It would not have been wise for me to be seen in his company.

Our conversation was not a long one, and it did happen a few years ago as I said, but I remember a lot of it—I remember because what he said has kept coming back to me again and again. Not that I understand fully what he meant—even now. He began by speaking about a need for some kind of rebirth—a rebirth that is necessary for one who seeks to enter the kingdom of God. Now, that kind of talk is certainly alien to any teaching I have ever heard in all my years of study. I challenged him by asking how that was possible. Once you are born, you can't go through the birth canal a second time, can you? But he pressed on by saying one must be born of water and the Spirit to enter the kingdom of God.

At the time it sounded so confusing—so totally different from anything I knew. I was completely confounded. But then he said something I remember almost word for word. He said, "Do not be astonished that I said to you, 'You must be born from above.' The wind blows where it chooses, and you hear the sound of it, but you do not know where it comes from or where it goes; so it is with everyone who is born of the Spirit." I remember that clearly. Maybe I remember it because I remember the chill wind that was blowing as we spoke. But over these years I have done some study of the Torah and the prophetic and poetic writings of the Scriptures, and that study has opened my eyes a little to the mysterious workings of the Spirit of God. I have few answers, and many questions still, but what may be part of the answer is that the Spirit (and perhaps this new birth Jesus talked about) gives us new eyes and a new heart and a new mind that open us to an alternative way of looking at our lives as people of God.

Since that day I have followed his career—from a distance, of course. What became more and more clear to me is that he lived out that new birth in his own life. I know of no instance where he ever did anything for his own gain. Indeed, in these last couple of days, he did nothing and said little even in his own defense at the mock trials that led up to his death. He risked everything to offer by his own example the kind of selflessness that could only mean that the principle upon which he moved put everything—life, death, reputation, honor—in the hands of God.

Perhaps . . . no, not perhaps. I have to say it here. That example is what led me to make a small sacrifice of my own for a principle. As I said before I am frightened to death of the future, but I did what I felt I had to do. I went to the market and bought the spices and carried them to the tomb where he was to be buried. I met my friend Joseph there—Joseph also has put himself at risk by asking for the body and for making his own tomb available. We prepared the body of Jesus for burial as best we could.

I have a confession to make. After the burial I was supposed to go home to celebrate the Passover, but I didn't go. That was a terrible thing to do—miss the celebration of the Passover. Instead, I went down to the banks of the river Kebar, not far from where I met Jesus that night years ago. I sat down by the river and wept. I wept for Jesus and for his death. I wept for myself and the judgment I would face by revealing myself as a sympathizer and, yes, as a disciple of Jesus. But as I sat there through the long night, the wind came up, and moved the still waters of the river into ripples. I fancied that it was the breath of the Spirit that moved the water, and I began to believe that it was the breath of the Spirit that had moved me.

I have no idea what the next days will bring, and to be honest, I'm anxious about that. But in another way I feel quite . . . free. Free. And I believe with all my heart that that feeling of freedom will stay with me as long as that mysterious breeze of the Spirit keeps moving me along.

You know, that's the same breeze that brought me here tonight. Do you feel it too?

John 3:1-15

Now there was a Pharisee named Nicodemus, a leader of the Jews. He came to Jesus by night and said to him, "Rabbi, we know that you are a teacher who has come from God; for no one can do these signs that you do apart from the presence of God." Jesus answered him, "Very truly, I tell you, no one can see the kingdom of God without being born from above." Nicodemus said to him, "How can anyone be born after having grown old? Can one enter a second time into the mother's womb and be born?" Jesus answered, "Very truly, I tell you, no one can enter the kingdom of God without being born of water and Spirit. What is born of the flesh is flesh, and what is born of the Spirit is spirit. Do not be astonished that I said to you, 'You must be born from above.' The wind blows where it chooses, and you hear the sound of it, but you do not know where it comes from or where it goes. So it is with everyone who is born of the Spirit." Nicodemus said to him, "How can these things be?" Jesus answered him, "Are you a teacher of Israel, and yet you do not understand these things?

"Very truly, I tell you, we speak of what we know and testify to what we have seen; yet you do not receive our testimony. If I have told you about earthly things and you do not believe, how can you believe if I tell you about heavenly things? No one has ascended into heaven except the one who descended from heaven, the Son of Man. And just as Moses lifted up the serpent in the wilderness, so must the Son of Man be lifted up, that whoever believes in him may have eternal life.

John 19:38-42

After these things, Joseph of Arimathea, who was a disciple of Jesus, though a secret one became of his fear of the Jews, asked Pilate to let him take away the body of Jesus. Pilate gave him permission; so he came and removed his body. Nicodemus, who had at first come to Jesus by night, also came, bringing a mixture of myrrh and aloes, weighing about a hundred pounds. They took the body of Jesus and wrapped it with the spices in linen cloths, according to the burial custom of the Jews. Now there was a garden in the place where he was crucified, and in the garden there was a new tomb in which no one had ever been laid. And so, because it was the Jewish day of Preparation, and the tomb was nearby, they laid Jesus there.

Questions for Reflection
and Discussion

1. In John 3:1-15, Nicodemus came to Jesus *by night* which implies that he did not want others to know about the visit. The two of them talked and Jesus' words seemed very difficult for Nicodemus. Why do you think he had such trouble understanding the idea of a new birth?

2. In John 19:38-42, we hear about Joseph of Arimathea (another secret disciple) and Nicodemus working together to care for the body of their friend Jesus. What gave these two secret followers the courage to do what they did?

3. Nicodemus and Joseph took a great risk in taking Jesus' body away from the place of crucifixion to Joseph's tomb. What are some of the risks Christians face for acting on their faith in this day and age?

4. Can you identify moments when it was difficult for you to speak out or act for the sake of your faith?

5. What can we do to grow in our willingness to be more courageous in speaking out in the name of Christ?

8

Judas
Based on Matthew 26:14-16, 47-49; 27:3-10

Isn't this ironic? You and I—here in church? How does it feel being in the same room with Judas? How comfortable are you worshiping with me? Will you go home feeling dirty?

I see my tracks have been thoroughly obscured over the years. Not much is known for sure and I guess I like that. What about my name? Does it mean "false one?" Or "liar?" Or "hypocrite?" Or "one from Kerioth?" Was it always a curse?

What about my story? Since I was the only real Judean in the group did I talk differently or look different from the others? Did I attend the Lord's Supper that night "in which he was betrayed?" Matthew, bless his heart, said I did. The others are not so sure.

Was I of nobility? Is that why I gravitated to the authorities? Did I have my fingers in the till? Did I sell him out for money? Thirty pieces of silver was a pitiful price. Don't you think I knew it only covered restitution for a killed slave? How did I die anyway? Did I hang? Did I fall and burst open? Did the money buy land like Matthew said or did I kill myself on it as in Acts?

Let me be clear: I'm not interested in providing answers. You wouldn't believe me anyway. I'm more interested in how you add it up. That the early church saw me equaling Satan is quite clear. What do you say?

What about my motives? Was it that Jesus was indifferent to many points of the law, that he associated with all the wrong people?

Was it that Jesus failed to manifest his power in the holy city Jerusalem after telling us again and again that he had come for a showdown? Was it that Jesus didn't strike decisively against the enemies of the nation as I wished he would? Did I force Jesus' hand into a fireworks display of power so that the religious and political authorities would be convinced of his messiahship? Did I finally become convinced that Jesus was a false messiah, misleading the people?

What is the issue?

You want to know why I did it. But *I* want to know how you justify judging me. If the church is God's grace free and unbridled, then show it to me. We are here to discover the impact of the cross on the life of Judas. Really! Remember me? I'm the other tragic and violent death during Holy Week. Who cried for me? I'm the one who crashed headlong into the cross. In so doing I have been convicted, found guilty in your eyes.

Wrestle with this, you who think God's grace is so great. Is it big enough to get in the last word after a suicide? I have heard that the church has said it is so. I'd like to believe you.

I remember the day Jesus reached out to include me in the twelve. I preached. I taught. I cast out demons. I lived it. I doubted just like the rest. I also believed it as best I could. None of us had it figured out before that last Passover. You people forever reread the passion story knowing the ending. Would that we had that benefit. We lived it forward in a very uncertain time. I ultimately made the Easter story possible. Did God finger me for that task only to throw me away? I admit I am not proud of what I have done. But don't you think Jesus knew who he was getting when he chose me?

Answer me this, you who are so proud of your faith: is God's grace big enough to deal with the shame and guilt of a deed ultimately regretted? I have heard that the church has said it is so. Can I believe you?

I lived long enough to realize that no one is without despair. I remember the dead, the lepers, the lame, the blind, the hungry, the dead and buried. I also remember the miracles of healing, cleansing, walking, seeing, filled stomachs, and life restored. I imagine you are no different than the folks of my time. Do you really entrust the broken edges and cruel reality of your life to Jesus as Lord? Or are you maybe wanting him for the gifts he has to give? I also saw another miracle, that miracle on the cross—the miracle that there was no miracle. God turned his back on Jesus and let him die.

Tell me then, is God's grace big enough to deal with despair? Is it really true that God meets people in their pain? I have heard that the church has said it is so. I want to believe you.

You question why I did it. And I want to know how you, the church, justify judging me or all the other Judases throughout the years. I know you are in the room tonight, though there are more who dare not show their faces in this august, religious group. I'm not the only betrayer.

Do you believe what you confess—that God's grace is big enough to deal with all sinners? Can that possibly leave room for being judgmental? I have heard the gospel say it shall not be so among you. Let me experience what you believe.

Answer me this: How strong is God's grace? Is it strong enough to cover senseless acts? Strong enough to right injustice? Strong enough to match events for which you ask "Why?" but receive no answer? Strong enough to cover the way you live? Strong enough to make forgiveness believable?

It's strange, but what I remember most is Jesus saying "The one who is forgiven much, loves much." You might think I'm on trial tonight but the way I figure it, you are on the witness stand. Judas is only listening.

So tell me. How powerful is God's love?

Matthew 26:14-16, 47-49; 27:3-10

Then one of the twelve, who was called Judas Iscariot, went to the chief priests and said, "What will you give me if I betray him to you?" They paid him thirty pieces of silver. And from that moment he began to look for an opportunity to betray him.

While he was still speaking, Judas, one of the twelve, arrived; with him was a large crowd with swords and clubs, from the chief priests and the elders of the people. Now the betrayer had given them a sign, saying, "The one I will kiss is the man; arrest him." At once he came up to Jesus and said, "Greetings, Rabbi!" and kissed him.

When Judas, his betrayer, saw that Jesus was condemned, he repented and brought back the thirty pieces of silver to the chief priests and the elders. He said, "I have sinned by betraying innocent blood." But they said, "What is that to us? See to it yourself."

Throwing down the pieces of silver in the temple, he departed; and he went and hanged himself. But the chief priests, taking the pieces of silver, said, "It is not lawful to put them into the treasury, since they are blood money." After conferring together, they used them to buy the potter's field as a place to bury foreigners. For this reason that field has been called the Field of Blood to this day. Then was fulfilled what had been spoken through the prophet Jeremiah, "And they took the thirty pieces of silver, the price of the one on whom a price had been set, on whom some of the people of Israel had set a price, and they gave them for the potter's field, as the Lord commanded me."

Questions for Reflection and Discussion

1. In these selections from Matthew 26 and 27, is the picture of Judas someone you feel sorry for, or someone you hate, or some feeling in between?

2. In the soliloquy, Judas challenges us who think God's grace is so great to see just what that means. Are there any preconditions or limits for God's grace?

3. Why is Judas so uncomfortable a character for us? Give several reasons.

4. Do you think God really consigned Judas to hell?

5. What gets in the way of the church's proclamation of forgiveness?

6. Is it a contradiction in terms for a Christian to be judgmental?

9

Mary Magdalene— Easter Morning
Based on John 20:1-18

Oh, I have such news. But I'm not sure if I should tell you. It's hard to know who to trust today. I mean, I'm sure that you wouldn't do anything to harm him—at least most of you wouldn't, but he did tell me to go and tell the others, and the news is so wonderful I can't hold it back any longer.

I've seen him! Yes, I've seen him! I have seen Jesus. He's alive! I know you probably think that I'm hallucinating, but I know I'm not. Jesus stood before me this morning as real as any one of you. And he talked to me! Oh, I know this all sounds hard to believe, but let me try and tell you what happened this morning. Maybe you can understand it.

I didn't sleep much last night. I haven't slept all week, really. This whole horrible nightmare has kept me twisting and turning every night. I've been so afraid. First for the Master and then— after Friday's horror—I was afraid for all of us. I tried to imagine how we could go on without him. I even tried to dream up a plan where we could continue to do his work—teaching and healing. But without him, it all seemed so futile. Without him, we already were beginning to fall apart, this silly little band of followers. None of us ever really understood very well. We didn't understand what he was trying to tell us. But since his death, his words have come back to me so often, and I am beginning to see some sense in it all. I guess I'm getting away from my story.

I gave up on sleep last night; actually, it must have been very early this morning. I got up quietly so as to not disturb the others and went out into the dark. Things look so different in the dark, don't they? All the comfort of familiar things gets lost in the blackness. I just stood there for a while, outside the door, not knowing which way to turn or where I wanted to go. And then I just started to walk. Where, I didn't seem to know or care—but not for long. I was headed in only one direction. To the tomb. Oh, I heard all of the warnings about not venturing out alone, staying with the others. We're not very popular right now, those of us who were his closest friends. But none of that seemed to matter once I was on the road leading to the tomb.

It was eerie and strange out there, yet I felt safe. Safe enough to travel the same road that we took on Friday to Golgotha. As I walked I could see that the sky was growing lighter. Black was giving way to the shadowy blue of dawn, and a thin line of sunlight rested on the horizon as though waiting for the exact moment when it would burst out over the earth. I couldn't understand it then, but my heart wasn't as heavy as it had been. And I wasn't so preoccupied with my grief. Instead, I walked into the night almost looking forward to something new, anxiously waiting for a new day. I didn't know what I'd do when I got to the tomb—I just knew I needed to be there.

But when I got there, my first thought was that I had taken a wrong turn. It didn't look like it had on Friday. Something was wrong. The stone from the front of the tomb had been taken away and I could see in the shadowy light the opening that led to the place where we laid him. But there was no body there! I couldn't believe it! I couldn't believe my own eyes! Jesus' body was gone. I was terrified! Who would do this? Why? Who would take his broken body from that place? The next thing I knew I was back on the road, this time running back toward home. The tears were running down my cheeks and stinging me with a kind of pain I have never known. I burst into the room where some of the others were and I screamed, "They have taken the Lord out of the tomb, and we do not know where they have laid him." I'll never forget the look on Peter's face, waking out of a sound sleep and hearing the news. Shock and horror shot through them all. John ran from the place, down the road, with Peter right behind him. I couldn't catch up to them but I followed. I wanted to be there. I wanted to know.

When they got to the tomb they hesitated for a moment, but then they went in and saw it just as I had said. The burial cloths were there on the ground, as though someone had uncovered him before they moved his body. Why? I kept asking myself. Why? Who would want to do this—to us? Is there so much hate about this man of love that they would play some horrid trick on us? I must admit that my thoughts were not loving. I was certain this was the work of the ones who had killed him.

John and Peter tried to convince me that there was nothing we could do there and that I should go home with them. But I couldn't leave that place. I couldn't move. Was it fear? Was it overwhelming sadness? I have no idea. All I know is that I just couldn't leave there. Reluctantly, they left me there after I promised to follow them shortly. I watched them walk away and then I went back to the tomb for one last glimpse.

Tears came easily, and I heard my own voice as though it were a stranger's, crying out all of the hurt and grief that was in me. But it wasn't enough for me to just stand outside, so I stooped down to get a better look into the tomb, my vision blurred by my own tears. What I saw there startled me. There were two of them—two men in white sitting right in the place where we had put Jesus' body. They looked harmless enough, two young men brilliantly dressed in white, shining robes. I wasn't afraid of them—I was fascinated. They spoke to me, asking me why I was crying. I blurted out the awful story of discovering that someone had taken Jesus' body away.

Just then, I turned away for a moment and out of the corner of my eye, I caught sight of someone standing behind me. I didn't recognize him, but I thought perhaps he was the gardener. My mind raced to the possibility that he had taken Jesus' body away. So when he asked about my weeping and wondered who I was looking for, I said to him if he knew where Jesus was to tell me and we would take care of the body. But instead, he turned toward me with a look that conveyed great tenderness and said my name in a way that I shall never forget. It was the Master's voice. I knew. No one else sounds like that. No one else says my name with such gentleness and care. It was as though all of my remembrance of who Jesus was to me was poured out again as I heard that voice call my name. I ran toward him and called out "Rabboni"—teacher. I looked at him and I wanted to cling to him and never, ever let him go again. But he stopped me. He motioned for me to stand away from him. And then he told me not to touch him. Oh, what hard words to hear. He must have known how difficult that moment was for me. First to recognize that he was no longer dead—to see a miracle before me—and then to be told not to touch, not to feel, not to hold him to me. I didn't understand. I didn't understand what he meant about 'ascending to the Father.' The only thing I knew in that moment was that some wonderful joke had been played on all of those people who had treated him so badly. I could not hold him, but neither could cruel death. He was out of the tomb and he was there in front of me—alive and standing in the light of day!

I don't know when it happened. I didn't see the sun slip above the edge of the horizon and stretch its rays into that forsaken place. I didn't see it until it had turned that tomb into a brilliant background for early morning light and shadows. It was morning and it was wonderful.

My feet flew down the path as I ran to tell the others in the morning sun. "I have seen the Lord!" I told them. They thought I had lost my mind—that I was too overwhelmed by my grief to know what was real any more. But my story did not change. It was true and one by one, most of them began to believe me, as strange and wonderful as it all was. I've just come from there now, and I told them the story just as I have told it to you. I know that some of them are still thinking that I'm too likely to get carried away by my imagination and that that's what this story is—something that I have made up but I know the truth. Jesus is alive. He is no longer buried in the tomb—Peter and John were witnesses to that. And even the doubters will come to believe it! Jesus has defeated death.

Even as I say it, I can feel the tears running down my cheeks. The truth is too wonderful to bear without remembering how awful we felt when we knew he was dead. He suffered and he died. I am not sure why or how this was his lot. But somehow, he knew it even before it happened. And now everything is paled by this marvelous news. It feels like a burden has been lifted. Everything seems new.

Now I have hope in me again. My heart beats with the rhythm of joy and I know that I will dance again and laugh again and love again. That's what Jesus has done for me. His life has brought me to life. He has given me hope. And he has touched me with his love.

Will I ever feel his touch again? A feeling in me says I won't, because something different is happening now. Yes, it is Jesus who I saw in the garden today—but something is quite different this time, and only he can tell us what all of it means. In time, I believe we will all understand. Yes, all of us. But strangely enough even the uncertainty doesn't frighten me this morning. Maybe it's because the light is so bright. Or the news is so wonderful. Or maybe it's because the truth that Jesus is alive has released me from my fears! Oh, what a morning this has been. What a wonderful, brilliant, joyful morning. And I, Mary Magdalene, who once lived life only in the shadows, I have heard him call my name in the glorious light of this new day.

John 20:1-18

Early on the first day of the week, while it was still dark, Mary Magdalene came to the tomb and saw that the stone had been removed from the tomb. So she ran and went to Simon Peter and the other disciple, the one whom Jesus loved, and said to them, "They have taken the Lord out of the tomb, and we do not know where they have laid him." Then Peter and the other disciple set out and went toward the tomb. The two were running together, but the other disciple outran Peter and reached the tomb first. He bent down to look in and saw the linen wrappings lying there, but he did not go in. Then Simon Peter came, following him, and went into the tomb. He saw the linen wrappings lying there, and the cloth that had been on Jesus' head, not lying with the linen wrappings but rolled up in a place by itself. Then the other disciple, who reached the tomb first, also went in, and he saw and believed; for as yet they did not understand the scripture, that he must rise from the dead. Then the disciples returned to their homes.

But Mary stood weeping outside the tomb. As she wept, she bent over to look into the tomb; and she saw two angels in white, sitting where the body of Jesus had been lying, one at the head and the other at the feet. They said to her, "Woman, why are you weeping?" She said to them, "They have taken away my Lord, and I do not know where they have laid him." When she had said this, she turned around and saw Jesus standing there, but she did not know that it was Jesus. Jesus said to her, "Woman, why are you weeping? Whom are you looking for?" Supposing him to be the gardener, she said to him, "Sir, if you have carried him away, tell me where you have laid him, and I will take him away." Jesus said to her, "Mary!" She

turned and said to him in Hebrew, "Rabbouni!" (which means Teacher). Jesus said to her, "Do not hold on to me, because I have not
yet ascended to the Father. But go to my brothers and say to them,
'I am ascending to my Father and your Father, to my God and your
God.' " Mary Magdalene went and announced to the disciples, "I
have seen the Lord"; and she told them that he had said these things
to her.

Questions for Reflection and Discussion

1. Why was hearing her name spoken by Jesus so important to Mary? She had already talked with him but his words before then had little effect on her.

2. How would you feel if someone who had just died who was dear to you was somehow alive again, healed and whole? Some of those feelings may very well have been part of Mary's experience.

3. Jesus' victory over death gives us hope and joy. How is your life different because of Easter?

4. In 1 Corinthians 15, the importance of Jesus' resurrection is emphasized. According to verses 35-44, how will our resurrection bodies be different than our present physical bodies?

5. One reason the Christian church changed the day of worship and rest from Saturday (the Sabbath) to Sunday is that Jesus' resurrection occurred on Sunday. How can each Sunday be a "little Easter" for you?

A Brief Worship Service

The Opening Dialogue:

LEADER: Grace and peace be multiplied to you in the knowledge of God and Jesus our Lord.

PEOPLE: Praised be God, the Father of our Lord Jesus Christ, the source of all mercies, and the God of all consolation.

LEADER: Seek the Lord while he may be found.

PEOPLE: Call upon him while he is near.

LEADER: Let the wicked abandon their ways,

PEOPLE: And the unrighteous their thoughts.

LEADER: Let them turn to the Lord for mercy,

PEOPLE: To our God, who is generous in forgiving.

LEADER: All you who are thirsty, come to the water. You who have no money, come, receive bread, and eat. Come, without paying and without cost, drink wine and milk.

PEOPLE: Praised be God, the Father of our Lord Jesus Christ, the source of all mercies, and the God of all consolation.
—Adapted from *LBW*, p. 127. Based on 2 Peter 1:2, 2 Corinthians 1:3, and Isaiah 55:1, 6.

The Opening Hymn

The Prayer of the Day

Scripture

Soliloquy

Hymn

The Offering

Litany for Lent

LEADER: For the sake of your tender mercy, O Lord, hear the prayers of your people who seek to honor you with lives and hearts devoted to your service.

67

PEOPLE: Give us strength for our journey, O Lord, that we may bear faithful witness to your never failing love. Keep us mindful of the great love with which you have loved us, so that in the power of that love we may find the courage to act on the strength that sustains us.

LEADER: At the cost of your great love we have been claimed as your people, and called to bear witness to your love for us and for your whole creation.

PEOPLE: Renew in us the assurance of your love so that in the complexities of our lives we may not falter in the face of uncertainty and doubt, but may abide in the consolation that your unconditional love gives us.

LEADER: Remind us each day that you are the source of all true wisdom, and restore in us the trust we need to face the changes and challenges of our lives with confidence.

PEOPLE: Grant to us, O Lord, a measure of your divine wisdom so that we may find the courage and hope we need to remain faithful to our calling as people of God, cherished and redeemed by your steadfast love.

LEADER: In your great and tender mercy, O Lord, bless us with the gifts for which we pray. Lord, remember us in your kingdom, and teach us to pray . . .

PEOPLE: OUR FATHER IN HEAVEN . . .

The Benediction

Prayers

The Centurion

O God, let us not be content to wait and see what will happen, but give us the determination to make the right things happen. While time is running out, save us from the patience which is akin to cowardice. Give us the courage to be either hot or cold, to stand for something, lest we fall for anything. In Jesus' Name. AMEN.

—A Prayer of Peter Marshall

Mary Magdalene

God be in my head, and in my understanding;
God be in my eyes, and in my looking;
God be in my mouth, and in my speaking;
God be in my heart, and in my thinking.
God be at mine end, and at my departing. AMEN.

—The Sarum Primer Prayer

Simon of Cyrene

Teach us, good Lord, to serve you as you deserve:
    To give and not count the cost;
    To fight and not heed the wounds;
    To toil and not seek for rest;
    To labor and not ask for reward,
    save that of knowing that we do your will;
through Jesus Christ our Lord. AMEN.

—A Prayer of Ignatius Loyola

Pilate's Wife

O God, you are the Light of the minds that know you,
the Life of the souls that love you, and the Strength of
the thoughts that seek you; help us so to know you, that
we may truly love you, so to love you that we may fully
serve you, whose service is perfect freedom; through Jesus
Christ our Lord. Amen.

—The Gelasian Sacramentary

Joseph of Arimathea

Give me the strength lightly to bear my joys and sorrows.
Give me the strength to make my love fruitful in service.
Give me the strength never to disown the poor or bend
my knee before insolent might.
Give me the strength to raise my mind above daily trifles.
And give me the strength to surrender my strength to
your will with love. AMEN.

—A Prayer of Rabindranath Tagore

Mary, the Mother of Jesus

O God, from whom to be turned is to fall,
to whom to be turned is to rise,
and in whom to stand is to abide forever;
Grant us
in all our duties your help;
in all our perplexities your guidance;
in all our dangers your protections;
and in all our sorrows your peace;
through Jesus Christ our Lord. AMEN.

—A Prayer of St. Augustine

Nicodemus

O God of time and eternity, who makes us creatures of time, to the end that when time is over, we may attain to your blessed eternity. With time, which is your gift, give us also wisdom to redeem the time lest our day of grace be lost, for the sake of Jesus Christ our Lord. AMEN.

—A Prayer of Christina Rossetti

Judas

O Lord, be gracious unto us! In all that we hear or see, in all that we say or do, be gracious unto us. We ask pardon of the great God. We ask pardon at sunset when every sinner turns to God. Now and forever we ask pardon of God. O Lord, cover us from our sins, guard our children, and protect our weaker friends. AMEN.

—The Bedouin Camel Drivers' Prayer at Sunset

(Adapted from William Barclay, *Epilogues and Prayers*, Abingdon Press, New York and Nashville, 1963.)